The New Playground

Written by Pam Bull

Illustrations by Jane Wallace-Mitchell

"Dad, we need
a new playground,"
said Matt.

2

Matt's dad said,
"I know what to do."

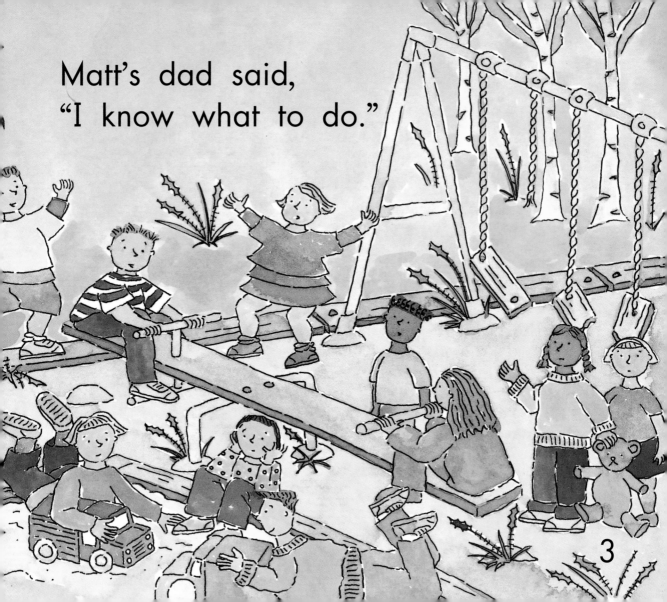

3

That Saturday,
moms and dads
came to the park.

4

Julia's mom brought the plan.

5

Jason's dad brought the wood.

Ken's mom brought the sand.

Jan's dad brought the tires.

Emma's dad brought the pipes.

9

Cindy's mom brought the paint.

10

11

Greg's mom brought plants.

Rick's dad brought a camera.

Maria's dad brought pizza.
Cory's mom brought
a trash can.

14

And Nancy's mom brought...

the kids!